On the Edge

Thrill Sports Poster Book

by Jeff Putnam

Willowisp
Press®

PHOTO CREDITS:

Front cover: Daredevil skiing–Eric Sanford/Tom Stack & Associates • Surfing–Vince Cavataio/Allsport USA • Rock climbing–Tim Defrisco/Allsport USA

Interior: Bungee jumping–Christian Schneider/Mountain Stock • White-water rafting–Robert W. Ginn/Unicorn Stock Photos • Rock climbing–Tim Defrisco/Allsport USA • Mountain biking–Mike Powell/Allsport • Skydiving–Francois Rickard/Allsport France • Hang gliding–G. Kalt/Leo de Wys, Inc. • Snow boarding–Monoski/Peter Arnold, Inc. • Ice climbing–Mike Powell/Allsport USA • Daredevil skiing–De Wys/Sipa/Lenz • Rodeo bull riding–Thomas Kitchin/Tom Stack & Associates • Shark diving–Jeffrey L. Rotman/Peter Arnold, Inc. • Surfing–Vince Cavataio/Allsport USA • Windsurfing–Eric Sanford/Tom Stack & Associates • Cliff diving–Steve Vidler/Leo de Wys, Inc.

Published by Willowisp Press, a division of PAGES, Inc. • 801 94th Avenue North, St. Petersburg, Florida 33702

Printed in the United States of America

2 4 6 8 10 9 7 5 3 1

ISBN 0-87406-709-X

BUNGEE JUMPING

Imagine diving off a bridge, cliff, tower, or even a hot-air balloon with only an elastic cord, called a *bungee*, tied around your feet. In free fall, you see the ground zooming up toward you at more than seventy terrifying miles an hour. The rush of the wind in your ears is all you can hear.

Then, right before you hit the ground, your world suddenly turns upside down. You bounce a hundred feet up in the air and keep on bouncing until you come to a stop. You've just made your first bungee jump.

Did You Know?

- The sport of bungee jumping got its start in the South Island of New Zealand, a small country southeast of Australia in the South Pacific Ocean.

- Operators of bungee jumps use science to make the sport safe. They weigh each jumper to determine how long to make the elastic bungee. Heavier jumpers get shorter cords. Lighter jumpers use longer cords.

WHITE-WATER RAFTING

They have names like Bloody Nose, Lost Paddle, Thread the Needle, and Heaven Help You. What are they? White-water rapids, or areas of very rough river water, that can empty a raft before the passengers know what hit them.

White-water rafting is popular all over the world. Led by a skilled guide, a small group of passengers paddles an inflated raft. They try their best to avoid rocks, cliffs, and nasty spills. Such groups often camp overnight by the river. Some rafting companies even make videotapes of the trips that passengers can buy.

Did You Know?

- Rapids are formed when a river drops quickly over a short distance. Lava Falls Rapid in the Grand Canyon drops thirty-seven feet over only sixty yards. Rapids often hide boulders and rocks that can tip a raft. Rafters classify rapids from class I, the easiest, to class VI, for experts only.

- Some of the most popular rafting rivers in the world are the Salmon River in Idaho, the Colorado River through the Grand Canyon in Arizona, the New and the Gauley rivers in West Virginia, and the Tatshenshini River in Canada. One of the most feared of all is the Bío-bío River in the Andes Mountains of Chile. It's full of class V rapids.

ROCK CLIMBING

There are a lot of different sports that might be called the fastest. But one of the slowest you'll ever find is rock climbing. Rock climbers have to take their time. They scale cliffs, looking for the tiniest handholds and cracks to place their feet in. Putting a hand or foot in the wrong place can mean a fall.

Rock climbers use lots of special equipment: ropes with special attachments for safety, *carabiners* (metal rings that attach to the ropes), climbing shoes, and helmets. Climbers also need to know some special knots for tying their ropes. Most rock climbers climb cliffs that are fifty feet high or less. But some experts climb much taller cliffs, as well as buildings, ridges, and towers.

Did You Know?

- Rock climbers prefer to climb cliffs made of hard rock. Cliffs made of soft rock, like sandstone, can crumble easily. Basalt, a smooth black rock, and granite, a very hard rock, are good for climbing.

- Yosemite National Park in California is the rock-climbing center of the United States. The ultimate challenge is the three-thousand-foot-high rock called El Capitan. The massive rock was scaled for the first time in 1958. It took the climbers fifty-six days to reach the top of El Capitan!

MOUNTAIN BIKING

Are you tired of riding your bike to school on tame city streets? Is it your idea of fun to navigate a bike through a stream, down a rocky canyon, or over a monster hill? Then mountain biking is for you.

Mountain bikes are rugged two-wheelers built to take extra punishment. They have fat, knobby tires for better traction, extra-strong frames, plenty of gears for climbing, and powerful brakes to stop riders before they plunge over a cliff. Mountain bikers also wear helmets, gloves, and goggles for added protection.

Did You Know?

- Bicycle gears help bikers peddle in different conditions. Low gears, which have the largest sprockets with more teeth, give more power for climbing hills. High gears, which have small sprockets and fewer teeth, supply speed for straightaways and cruising.

- The American West, with its wide open spaces and rugged landscapes, is popular mountain-biking territory. There's even a cross-country TransAmerica Trail that runs from Oregon to Virginia.

SKYDIVING

Do you know how fast traveling 174 feet per second is? It's 104 miles an hour, the top speed of many cars. It's also the speed you can reach when you jump out of an airplane, before you pull the ripcord that opens your parachute.

Many people have taken skydiving courses and have made their first jumps. A special kind of parachute, called a *parafoil*, lets the skydiver steer by pulling on nylon lines connected to the ends of the parafoil. *Skysurfing*, where a skydiver does maneuvers on a small surfboard during free fall, is also becoming popular.

Did You Know?

- The idea of the parachute has been around for thousands of years. A Chinese emperor in 90 B.C. tied straw hats together to try to float to the ground. Italian inventor Leonardo da Vinci designed a parachute in the 1500s. Today parachutes are big enough to lower a 180,000-pound rocket safely to the ground.

- Two French brothers, the Montgolfiers, are known as the fathers of hot-air ballooning. In the late 1700s, they lowered a sheep attached to a parachute from a tower.

HANG GLIDING

Have you ever looked at a hawk or sea gull soaring in the air and wished you could do the same? Get into hang gliding and you'll be able to soar like an eagle.

A hang glider is a large kite with a harness attached underneath for holding a person. Rising currents of warm air called *thermals* lift the glider into the air and keep it from falling. Strong thermals can lift a hang glider more than one thousand feet a minute. Pilots steer by shifting their body weight against steel tubes attached to the glider.

Did You Know?

- Hang gliding, like hot-air ballooning, is possible because hot air rises. If you look above a lighted match or another source of intense heat, you'll see that things look wavy. This is a result of the hot air around the heat source rising.

- The world championships of hang gliding are held in California's Sierra Nevada mountain range between Yosemite National Park and Mt. Whitney. The rugged peaks offer plenty of thermals for hang gliders to ride as they race around a one-hundred-mile course. Winners can navigate the course in about three and a half hours.

SNOW BOARDING

When the snow falls, some shredheads just can't wait to hop on their shred sleds, head for the half-pipe, and start practicing their crails, fakies, nose wheelies, and stale fish. The one thing they don't want to be is road pizza.

These people are snow boarders, and their sport is a wild mix of skiing, surfing, and skateboarding. The half-pipe is a tubelike trail with high, curving, snow-packed walls. Snow boarders can also race in a slalom, where they try to complete a course marked with flags. Crails, fakies, and the others are trick moves to make on a snow board. And road pizza is what you are after an especially bad fall!

Did You Know?

- Both snow boarders and skiers need one thing to practice their sports—snow. If nature supplies it, that's great. But if it doesn't, ski resorts can make their own snow as long as the weather is cold enough. Snow makers work by spraying tiny particles into the air. These particles attract ice crystals and fall to the ground as snow.

- When snow boarding first caught on, many ski resorts did not allow the sport. Now, most resorts offer special ski runs for snow boarders. Some of the most popular ski resorts in the United States are in the Rocky Mountains of Colorado and in the smaller Green Mountains of Vermont. Both areas usually get plenty of snow.

ICE CLIMBING

If you've ever slipped on a patch of ice, you might wonder why anybody would want to climb a one-hundred-foot frozen waterfall. But for ice climbers, it's the ultimate challenge.

Ice climbers need a lot of special equipment. They use rope and special screws that they insert into the ice. They attach steel rings called *carabiners* to the ice screws. They also use ice axes to pull themselves up and wear *crampons,* or long sharp metal cleats, on their boots. Ice climbing can be very dangerous, especially when temperature shifts make ice crack apart or cause avalanches.

Did You Know?

- Many ice climbers enjoy hiking on glaciers. Glaciers are huge masses of slowly moving ice that advance and retreat depending on the climate. As recently as ten thousand years ago, glaciers covered most of the northern United States and Canada.

- The Yatsugatake Mountains in central Japan are popular for ice climbing. The waterfalls and cliffs attract people from nearby Tokyo.

DAREDEVIL SKIING

How would you describe a person who trains for his sport by standing on the roof of a car going 140 miles per hour? You'd probably call him crazy. But others would call him a speed skier. Speed skiing is a type of daredevil skiing where the whole idea is simply to go downhill as fast as you can. The winner in an Olympic demonstration reached 142 miles an hour. Another skier was clocked at only 103 mph—but that was after he had fallen and was rolling down the hill!

Other types of daredevil skiing include freestyle aerial, where the skiers turn somersaults and do flips in midair, or skiing down rocky mountain sides without snow. There's also wilderness skiing, where skiers are helicoptered into isolated mountain ranges where no one has ever skied before.

Did You Know?

- There are several different ways to measure how fast something is moving. In the United States, the most familiar way is in miles per hour. But people in most parts of the world use the metric system. The Olympic skier who went 142 miles an hour was doing 229 kilometers an hour. To find his speed in feet per second, multiply 142 times 5,280. Then divide the total by 60 and then by 60 again.

- One of the world hot spots for daredevil skiing is the Alps mountain range in Europe. The Alps include parts of seven different countries: France, Germany, Italy, Switzerland, Austria, Liechtenstein, and Slovenia. The highest peak in the Alps is Mont Blanc in France.

RODEO BULL RIDING

Who would you choose as the roughest, toughest athletes of all? It would be hard to find anybody tougher than a rodeo cowboy. And the toughest cowboys of all are the ones who ride the bulls.

Think you could do it? All you have to do is sit for eight seconds on one angry ton of bucking, rearing bull who'd like nothing better than to toss you a country mile. You can hold on with one hand to an unknotted rope that goes around the bull's belly. But you'll be disqualified if that hand touches the bull. And watch out for the horns and the hooves—hundreds of cowboys have been seriously injured or killed riding the bulls.

Did You Know?

- Rodeo bull riders usually ride Brahman bulls, which originally came from India. They're considered the most difficult of all bulls to ride.

- Bull riding is one of many different events in a rodeo. Other rodeo events include calf roping, saddle bronc riding, and steer wrestling. These events are based on the activities of the cowboys who settled the western range in the 1800s. Two of the biggest rodeos today are the professional championships in Las Vegas, Nevada, and the Calgary Stampede in Calgary, Alberta.

SHARK DIVING

All adventure sports take guts. But how would it feel to be separated from 1,500 pounds of pure terror by a small steel cage? That's the incredible thrill a shark diver is looking for.

A few brave people wearing scuba diving gear are lowered into the ocean in a shark-proof cage. This allows them to get a close look at nature's most perfect killer. Shark divers can come face to face with a bull shark, tiger shark, hammerhead, or, most terrifying of all, the great white.

Did You Know?

- There are about 350 different kinds of sharks. They range in size from tiny to the gigantic whale shark, the biggest fish in the ocean. Only about 40 kinds of sharks have ever attacked people. The most feared shark is the great white. It averages 1,500 pounds and 15 feet, but the largest ever found was 25 feet long!

- Sharks are found in warm waters all over the world, including the east and west coasts of the United States, Australia, and South Africa. The worst shark attack ever was in Somalia on the east coast of Africa. At least forty people were killed in that unusual incident.

SURFING

Who hasn't dreamed about living a surfer's life, traveling the world in search of the perfect wave? Slipping down the front of a wave at thirty-five miles an hour or tube-riding the inside of a giant curl is tough to beat for thrills and chills.

Surfing is a way of life for lots of people, but it's a professional sport as well. Pro surfers compete for thousands of dollars in dozens of tournaments, where they're judged on their control and creativity.

Did You Know?

- Waves, the one thing a surfer can't live without, are created by wind blowing over large areas of water. Stronger winds and larger areas of water make bigger waves. The biggest waves surfers usually tangle with are about 10 feet high. The largest wave ever measured was 112 feet high, seen by a U.S. Navy ship in 1933. That monster wave was as tall as an eleven-story building!

- Many people think first of southern California when they think of surfing. But other surfing hot spots around the world are the coasts of Australia, where many world champions got their start, Mexico's Todos Santos, and Hawaii's famous beaches, including the legendary Banzai Pipeline.

WINDSURFING

It's one of the newest Olympic sports. But to *boardheads*—windsurfers who can't seem to think about anything else—windsurfing is more than a sport. It's a way of life. Back in 1967, a couple of surfers wondered if it might be possible to surf using a wind sail. The rest is history.

Today more than one and a half million people windsurf. A mast and sail are attached to a surfboard. The windsurfer stands on the board and steers by moving the sail around to catch the wind. Some windsurfers race each other around a course. Others prefer freestyle, in which they do acrobatic stunts—including flips. Some windsurfing tournaments are even held indoors in large pools. The winds are supplied by huge industrial fans.

Did You Know?

- Winds are caused by the uneven heating of the earth's atmosphere by the sun. Air above hot areas rises. Air from cooler areas moves into these areas, and the result is wind. Winds are always named for the direction they blow from. A north wind blows from the north to the south. A westerly wind blows from the west to the east.

- In 1990, a seventeen-year-old Cuban windsurfer used his board to escape from Cuba by sailing to Florida. He was sixty miles into his ninety-mile journey across the Straits of Florida when he was picked up by a passing freighter. The Coast Guard took the boy to Miami, where he was reunited with his

CLIFF DIVING

Chances are you've seen people dive off the high board at the swimming pool. Maybe you've even done it yourself. That diving board is usually about ten feet, or three meters, high. Plenty high enough for most people. But not for some.

Cliff divers like their diving platforms to be a little higher—about twelve times higher, to be exact. The famous cliff divers at La Quebrada cliffs in Acapulco, Mexico, hurl themselves headfirst off a platform that is 120 feet (37 meters) above a rocky sea cove. And that's not all. There's a little problem with waves surging in and out. When the waves rush out of the cove, the water is too shallow for diving. The cliff divers of Acapulco have to time their dives perfectly so that the waves are in when they hit the water. If their timing isn't perfect, their diving days are over.

Did You Know?

- A cliff diver is affected by the earth's gravity, a force that pulls bodies downward toward the earth. It's the same force that keeps the moon in orbit around the earth. Gravity was first explained by Sir Isaac Newton (1642-1727), an English scientist.

- Acapulco is a beautiful resort city on Mexico's Pacific coast, about two hundred miles southwest of Mexico City. Spanish explorers founded the city on the site of an old Indian village. Today Acapulco is famous as a busy vacation spot for thousands of tourists from all over the world.